Painting
as Prayer

Painting as Prayer

The Art of
A. Sophrony Sakharov

by

Sister Gabriela

PAINTING AS PRAYER
The Art of A. Sophrony Sakharov
by Sister Gabriela

First edition of 1000 (2017)
ISBN paperback edition: 978-1-909649-33-0
© 2019 The Stavropegic Monastery of St John the Baptist, Tolleshunt Knights, Essex CM9 8EZ, UK
ISBN hardback edition: 978-1-909649-12-5
© 2017 The Stavropegic Monastery of St John the Baptist, Tolleshunt Knights, Essex CM9 8EZ, UK

Published by
The Stavropegic Monastery of St John the Baptist, Tolleshunt Knights, Essex CM9 8EZ, UK

All photographs by Mark Edwards (info@markedwardsphotography.com) except:
pages 112, 113, 116, 118, 119, 174 by Robert Cotton
and page 175 by Katie Donnelly (kldphotography.co.uk)
and pages 6, 134, 135, 138, 139, 149, 150, 151, 158–161 (except three central images on 160–161
by Mark Edwards), 180 by Community of St John the Baptist

Design by mikestonelake.com

Cover illustration Drawing of the Holy Trinity, Son, mid/late 1970s

CONTENTS

Introduction   9

Creativity, Freedom and the Icon   11

COLOUR PLATES

Drawings   18

Murals   76

   Refectory   78

   St Silouan's Chapel   102

Panel Icons   130

Design   152

Biography   177

Father Sophrony's techniques   179

Notes on the illustrations   185

← A. Sophrony painting,
  early 1960s

Icons can be painted as a craft, and this is good, one can pray in front of these, but icons can also be art, and it is this quality that we should strive after.

INTRODUCTION

Art has the ability to touch that inner part of man and convey directly a creative experience and response difficult to express in words. It was the life long vocation of A. Sophrony (Sakharov)[1] (1896-1993) to offer this living experience through art. His artistic training had its roots in both Imperial and Soviet Russia where as a young student, he was influenced by the writings of Kandinsky on the spiritual in art. It was the spiritual life that called him ever more strongly and after working as a portrait and landscape artist in Paris, Father Sophrony abandoned his painting to become a monk on Mount Athos. Several decades later he moved to England, founding a monastery in the Essex countryside where again he took up painting, now in iconography, to provide for the needs of his monastery. Here he drew on all his earlier artistic knowledge to express in a unique way his own rich spiritual life and monastic experience.

Most of the subject matter of this book presents preparatory drawings, studies and sketches for wall paintings, followed by the paintings themselves, both murals and panel icons. The final section comprises his work on designs in various forms.

In 1983 I became part of the group assisting him with the murals painted in the Chapel. While we were working, Father Sophrony described two approaches to finishing a painting. The first, to paint in order for the work to be viewed from a distance. The second was to paint in such detail that it could be appreciated both from a distance and at close quarters enabling it also to be favourably photographed. Father Sophrony was aiming for the second method as is evident in all the initial preparatory drawings and studies. However even when seeing the work at first hand, the finer details may often pass unnoticed either because of distance or because they are lost in the overall composition.

It is my intention to publish a complete catalogue of all of Father Sophrony's work but as this will be a long and involved undertaking I resolved to publish something from the collection of which this first book offers a small selection.

Sr Gabriela

---

[1] Though his ecclesiastic title is Archimandrite, I have referred to him as Father Sophrony in the text which is how he was known and addressed in his Community.

CREATIVITY, FREEDOM AND THE ICON

This world ... hides from view the Beautiful Face of God. God does not act by force; He holds sacred the freedom of those created in His image and likeness.[1]

How then may one represent the face of God hidden by the world? The most direct way to form an image of God is through the heart, the meeting place between God and man,[2] but this remains a personal and hidden form. There is a visual path to the heart, which is the way of the icon.[3] The work of the icon is to portray His face and offer it to the world. It is to be a bridge between the secular and the spiritual, the earthly and the heavenly, to bring people to the knowledge of God. This search for the knowledge of God was the entire endeavour of Father Sophrony's life and it found expression in his art.

Freedom is indispensable for any true creation. God created man free and respects this freedom absolutely. Only what is offered freely has any value and in this aspect it is a necessary condition for any true creativity, be it painting, music, poetry, sculpture or writing. The artist has to be free to listen to the quiet voice of inspiration, coming from outside or from within. To catch inspiration from without requires a keen sense of perception and receptivity, while inner inspiration is found when the artist fathoms the very depths of his[4] soul, exposing the desire and necessity to create and give shape or sound to the seeds hidden or discovered there. As Tolstoy expresses it,

> Art is a microscope which the artist fixes on the secrets of his soul, and shows to people these secrets which are common to all.[5]

However to disclose "the secrets of one's soul" requires discernment as not every thing from either outside or within is worthy or appropriate to be represented. The artist feels intuitively what may be expressed and when to keep silent; what should be revealed and what remain hidden. Because the visual has a strong impact this requires great care. A Russian painter of the 19th century describes the inner state of the artist,

---

[1] A. Sophrony, *Letters to his Family*, Tolleshunt Knights: Stavropegic Monastery of St. John the Baptist, 2015, p. 198.

[2] Cf. St Paul: "For God who commanded the light to shine out of darkness, hath shined in our hearts, to give the light of the knowledge of the glory of God in the face of Jesus Christ." (2 Cor 4:6).

[3] By "icon" the Christian Eastern icon is meant, not just any image.

[4] Artists are obviously both male and female. For clarity and simplicity in the text I refer to the artist as masculine.

[5] Tolstoy, diary entry May 1896.

An artist is a person who believes with deep conviction in the rightness of what he creates; who devotes his entire life to art for mankind. Only in such people does the Divine spark burn, brightly and unquenchably. And this is what's most important in art. Where the soul ceases there death begins.[6]

Again, this applies to all the arts, but in the case of painting, the possibilities narrow down; it is by nature less ethereal than music, and also to a certain extent, than poetry. A painting consists of matter and this material has to be transformed into art. The artist is like the conductor of an orchestra who directs the sounds to interpret the music, but in the case of the painter, the "sounds" are visible colours. These he needs to organize into a shape and form that convey what he wants to say.

For a painting to be good it has to have an aim and a purpose; it can rarely be acceptable as just an impression. One of Father Sophrony's teachers observes,

> Painting is an art. Art is not the senseless creation of things, diffused in a vacuum. It is a powerful force and has many aims. It should serve the development and refinement of the human soul. … Art is a language whereby we speak to the soul (in a form accessible and peculiar only to this language) of things which are the soul's daily bread and which it can acquire only in this form.[7]

For a painting to have a full and serious meaning, it requires its own inner life with a message and a purpose. Without this it stays just a pretty picture, an external description and an empty shell. It may be composed of nice colours and good forms but it leaves the onlooker empty, or at best, it may please the aesthetic senses but fails to create a deeper resonance within. It remains superficial and the spectator is left untouched.

The inner life that will resonate with the onlooker needs the kind of inspiration mentioned above and the artist must be all attention to catch it and transmit it in its purest and most honest form. Kandinsky writes,

> [the artist] must not consider himself master of the situation, but the servant of nobler aims – a servant whose obligations are majestic, distinctive, and sacred. He must nurture himself and plumb the depths of his inner life, he must conserve his inner life and develop it lest his outer talent becomes empty, like a lost glove, the empty and vain likeness of a hand.[8]

There is a stage in creation where the artist feels as if the work happens of its own accord, that he is merely a servant of another dynamic and strength. Here he needs to be careful and not let himself get lost in a senseless wave of inspiration. It requires a certain critical temperance

---

6 Mark Antokol'skii, *Letter to Stasov*, Experiment, Vol. 14, Los Angeles, 2008, page 162.

7 V. Kandinsky, *On the Spiritual in Art (1920)*, Experiment, Vol. 8, Los Angeles, 2002, page 113.

8 *Ibid*, page 114.

and emphasizes the need for an inner life from which to judge how and what is to be painted. The artist has a great responsibility, as his role is to reveal and show deeper things, to give meaning to his art. To prepare himself he needs to cultivate his spiritual life and develop it so that it becomes attuned and receptive to inspiration, while at the same time taking responsibility for his creation.

This brings us back to Kandinsky's view that the artist needs to have an inner life, to speak to the soul of the onlooker and evoke a response within him. This is necessary for all art but in the Christian Orthodox icon, where the aim is to represent the hidden face of God, it all takes a step further.

The icon is an art which expresses the spiritual world in form and colour. It is made with a stylistic language of its own which introduces the person looking at it into another sphere of being, another world of perception. Intentionally it follows a different logic of perspective and reality, placing emphasis on the inner life because it's main purpose is either to depict the face of God or convey the soul of the Saint or the essence of the scene depicted. Deliberately this makes it somewhat abstract. The artist seeks Divine inspiration for his work and in order to receive this, rather than some other influence, he needs a humble and prayerful attitude, recognizing that he is not master of the situation.

> Inspiration from on High depends to a considerable extent on us – on whether we open our heart so that the Lord – the Holy Spirit Who 'stands at the door and knocks' – does not have to enter forcibly … The Lord preserves the freedom of those created 'in His image'.[9]

The iconographer will try to free himself from all that hinders or is contrary to the action of Divine inspiration. This requires both humility and asceticism, but as ascetic feats may lead to pride, and thus deter grace, it is humility that is the essential part. This keeps him open both to others and their suggestions and open to grace. It preserves a rigorous questioning and checking in prayer with his conscience and with the ideal which is the humble example of Christ.

> Christ-like humility is an all-conquering force. It knows no degradation. It is divinely majestic.[10]

This Divine humility is unattainable on earth, but in striving towards it and revealing one's inner thoughts and states to one with greater experience in the spiritual life, a fuller understanding may be reached. The iconographer aims to humble himself, giving place for grace to act so that he becomes a servant or assistant of the icon that is created rather than its creator.

---

[9] A. Sophrony, *We Shall See Him As He Is*, Tolleshunt Knights: Stavropegic Monastery of Saint John the Baptist, 1988, page 120.

[10] A. Sophrony, *On Prayer*, Tolleshunt Knights: Stavropegic Monastery of Saint John the Baptist, 1996, page 15.

The natural world is so arranged that man is constantly faced with problems to which he must seek solutions. But in order truly to work with God in the creation of the world man must ever aspire to the utmost possible knowledge of God Himself. The continual climb towards further and further knowledge of God is also a creative act, though of an especial order.[11]

In Father Sophrony's case this climb towards further knowledge of God and learning creativity through Him took a roundabout way. From a young age he had dedicated his life to art. Painting was everything for him. His way of perceiving the world was through the eyes of a painter, his reactions and expressions all passed through the prism of painting. From childhood he had been keenly interested in eternity and what happens after death, so it was natural for him to seek solutions through his art. It was in this search for the eternal that for a few years he abandoned his childhood Christian faith and devoted himself to eastern mysticism, thinking that this would lead him to further and fuller truths. In addition, he came under the influence of the writings and art of Kandinsky and entered the world of abstraction. For a short while he exercised himself on this path until it became apparent that it did not solve his questions and led to a void.

Just as every artist apprehends objective reality through the forms and modes of his art, so I derived ideas of my abstract studies from life around me. I would look at a man, a house, a plant, at intricate machinery, extravagant shadowscapes on walls and ceilings, at quivering bonfire flames, and would compose them into abstract pictures, creating in my imagination visions that were not like actual reality. This was how I interpreted the teaching of my master – not to copy natural phenomena but to produce new pictorial facts. Fortunately I soon realized that it was not given to me, a human being, to create from 'nothing', in the way God can create. I realized that everything that I created was conditioned by what was already in existence. I could not invent a new colour or line that had never existed anywhere before. An abstract picture is like a string of words, beautiful and sonorous in themselves, perhaps, but never expressing a complete thought. In short, an abstract picture represented a disintegration of being, a falling into the void, a return to the *non esse* from which we had been called by the creative act of God.[12]

The transition was not simple, it took much time and strength, often to the point of even disagreeing with God and not seeing the sense of His way of creating.

Unable to understand myself, weary of endless conflict and insoluble contradictions, I tried the experiment of putting myself in the Creator's place, and pondered how I would have ordered the world. Shutting myself up in the dark and quiet, I concentrated my thoughts on the task. Starting from my own experience of being, and keeping in mind the difficulties that constantly beset me,

---

[11] A. Sophrony, *Wisdom from Mount Athos*, Crestwood: St. Vladimir's Seminary Press, 1974, page 13.

[12] *Ibid*, pages 13–14.

I proceeded from the ephemeral to the ever-widening horizons of cosmic being. And what happened? Instead of rectifying the 'incoherencies' in God's work I soon found myself marvelling at the Mind which had created heaven and earth with such 'know-how' ... My soul overflowed with wonder at the unfathomable wisdom of God. Somewhere far away in the vast heavens a faint Light shone, inspiring songs of praise and begetting a hunger in me to be associated with the great creative work of the Father. (Sometimes when I was engaged in landscape painting people would come and stand quietly behind me, watching me work. In the same way I wanted to stand close to the Almighty and delight in contemplating His creative inspiration.)[13]

As this vision dawned on him he abandoned his art and set out to gain fuller knowledge of God and a greater understanding of true creativity from Him. After long years dedicated to prayer, the circumstances of Father Sophrony's life changed and he took up painting again. Now he was able to bring the fruit of all he had learned from his spiritual experience while drawing upon the wide knowledge he had gained as a young artist. With this he embraced the great tradition of iconography yet continued to enlarge his own creative vision.

Every icon was imbued with prayer and each new idea was submitted to careful testing as to whether it conformed to sacred tradition. Father Sophrony embraced the language of the iconographic tradition with all his heart, choosing it as the most suitable way of expressing the spiritual world. However this did not constrain his freedom and his creative spirit was ever awake within the framework of the icon, always keeping a personal touch, as in any form of creation, every artist tends to leave a trace of himself in his work. The icon in particular has to convey the inner life and energy of its subject and that trace from the artist becomes transformed by prayer into the icon's unique life. Through line and colour this inner life is communicated to the person praying in front of the image and resounds deeply in his soul.

In the utmost intensity of prayer that our nature is capable of, when God Himself prays in us, man receives a vision of God that is beyond any image whatsoever.[14]

[13] *We Shall See Him*, page 151.

[14] *Ibid*, page 195.

ne has to know the technique but also the art.
A good icon is like a painting.
Like a prayer written with beautiful letters.
With such an icon one can live all one's life
and just by looking at it one changes.

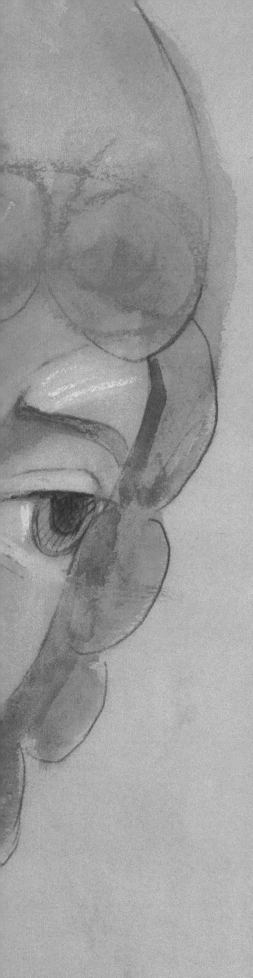

DRAWINGS

Before starting a painting, whether for a wall or panel, Father Sophrony drew studies on paper. Often several ideas and configurations were tried before a final decision was made.

For a full commentary on each drawing, refer to pages 185 to 188.

→ Christ, study for Christ in Glory

← Christ, Resurrection, Refectory

↘ Christ, Deisis, Refectory

↖ Christ, sketch for
Christ in Glory

→ Christ, Iconostasis,
St Silouan's Chapel

← Trinity, Father, Refectory

↘ Trinity, Father, Refectory

↙ Angel, Empty Tomb

↘ Trinity, Son

← Angel, Symbol
  of St Matthew

↖ Eagle, Symbol
  of St John

↙ Eagle, Symbol of St John
(reverse of drawing on
page 31)

↘ Lion, Symbol of St Mark

33

← Seraphim, detail of
  Christ in Glory

↘ Seraphim

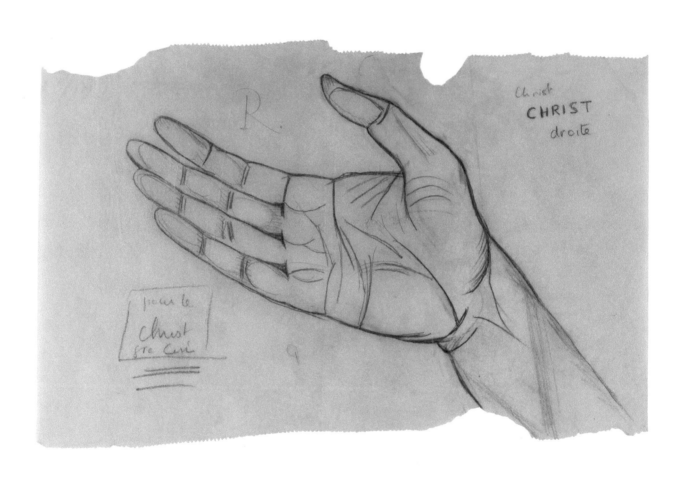

40

↙ Right hand of Christ, Last
Supper, St Silouan's Chapel

↘ Christ, Left hand

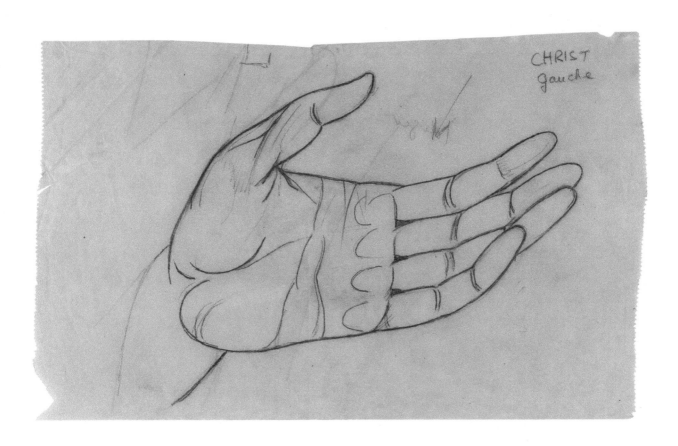

↙ Hand of Mother of
God at the Cross,
St Silouan's Chapel

→ Hand of Apostle,
Last Supper,
St Silouan's Chapel

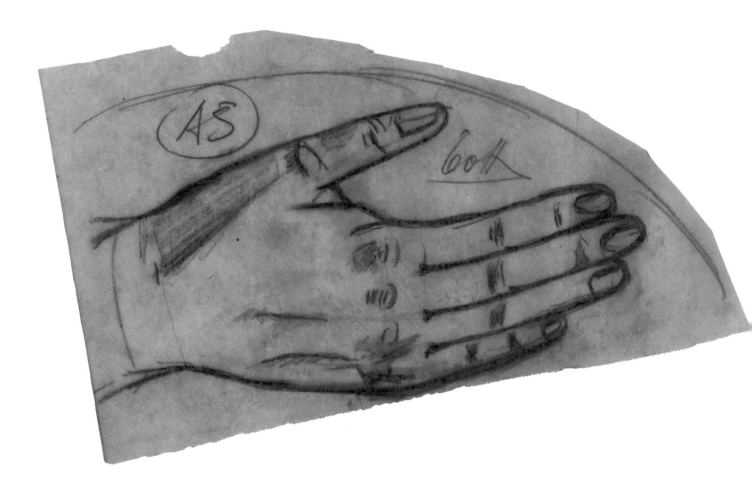

St Cène.

PHILIP.

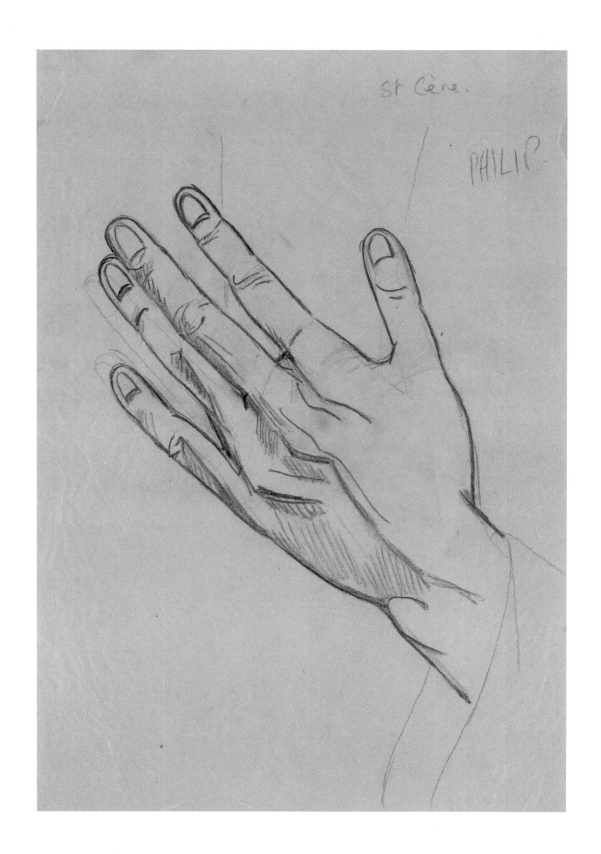

← Legs and feet of Prophet Moses

↘ Moses receiving the Law

Dessin pour Sophie
1er Août

← Mother of God
   at the Cross

↗ Christ, Crucifixion

St Jean
Croix
utilisé

← Adam

→ Eve

Adam
Resurrection
utilisé

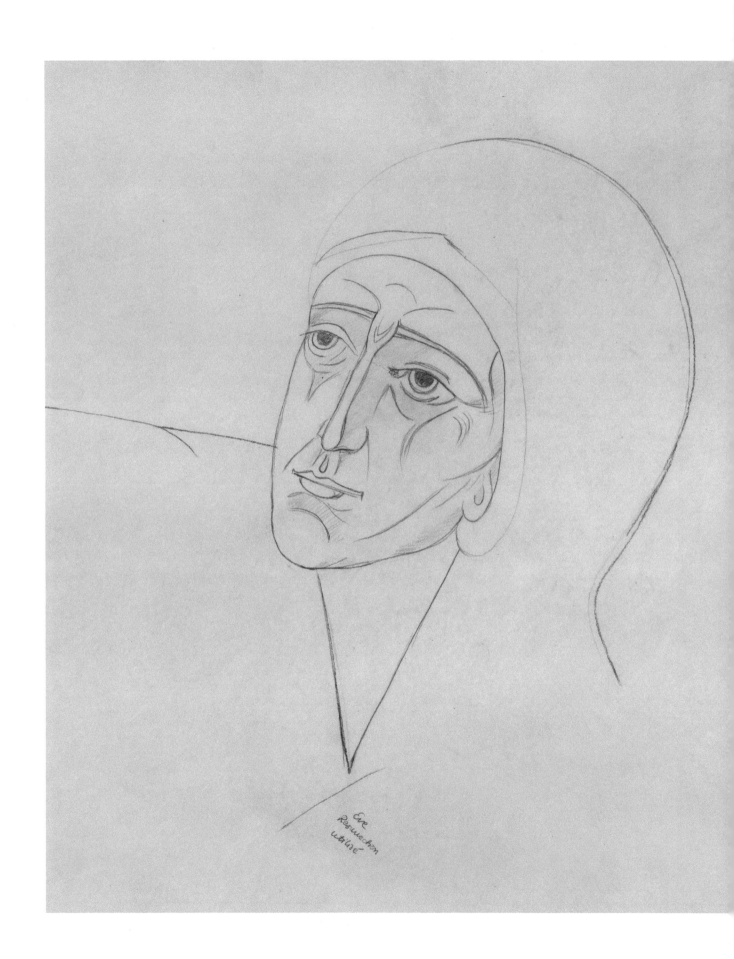

↘ St Helen

↘ St Helen

↓ St Helen, (reverse of drawing on page 55)

→ St Andrew

HAYM
OHRID

58

← St Naum

→ St Sophrony,
  Patriarch of Jerusalem

← St Silouan the Athonite,
St Silouan's Chapel

→ St Silouan, Refectory

← St Zacharias

↘ St Zacharias

↙ St James of Zebedee, Last Supper, Refectory

→ St Matthew, Last Supper, Refectory

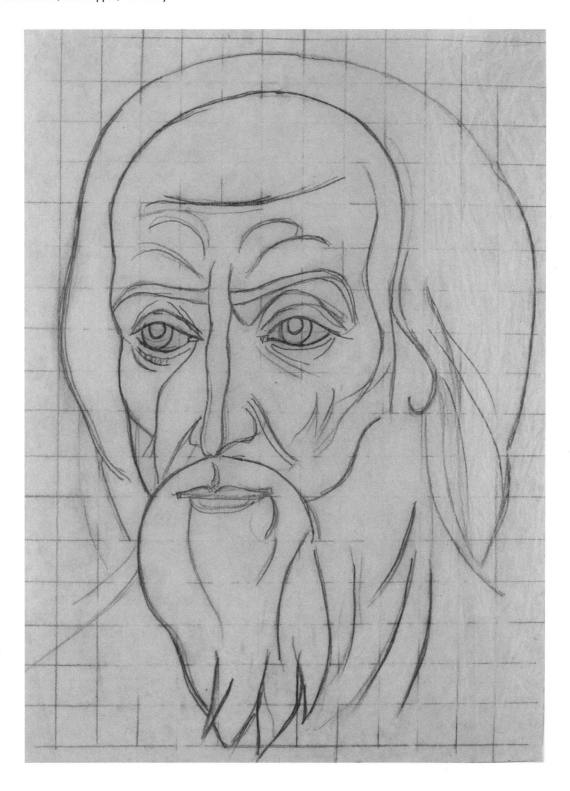

← St Bartholomew, Last Supper, Refectory

↘ St Peter, Last Supper, Refectory

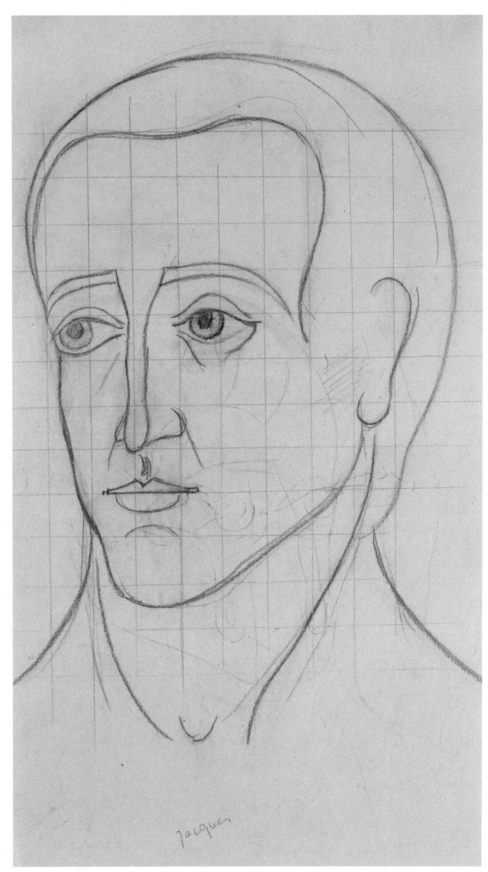

← St Paul,
  St Silouan's Chapel

→ St James of Alpheus,
  Refectory

← St Bartholomew,
  Last Supper, Refectory

→ St James of Zebedee,
  Last Supper, St Silouan's Chapel

← St Thomas, Last
   Supper, Refectory

→ St Philip, Last
   Supper, Refectory

MURALS

Two projects of murals are illustrated here: one for the Refectory of the Community of St John the Baptist, painted in the mid/late 1970s and early 1980s, and one for the Chapel of St Silouan, painted in the mid 1980s. The painting program for the Refectory was laid out so that the room could also serve as a place of worship. However in the early 1980s, it became possible to construct a proper chapel and there was a pause in the work on the walls of the Refectory.[1] The same wall painting program was repeated for the Chapel, yet the technique had evolved and one can see a distinct difference mainly in the treatment of the faces.

For a full commentary on each painting, refer to pages 188 to 191, and for a description of techniques, refer to pages 179 to 182.

[1] These were completed in the early 1990s, after the consecration of the Chapel.

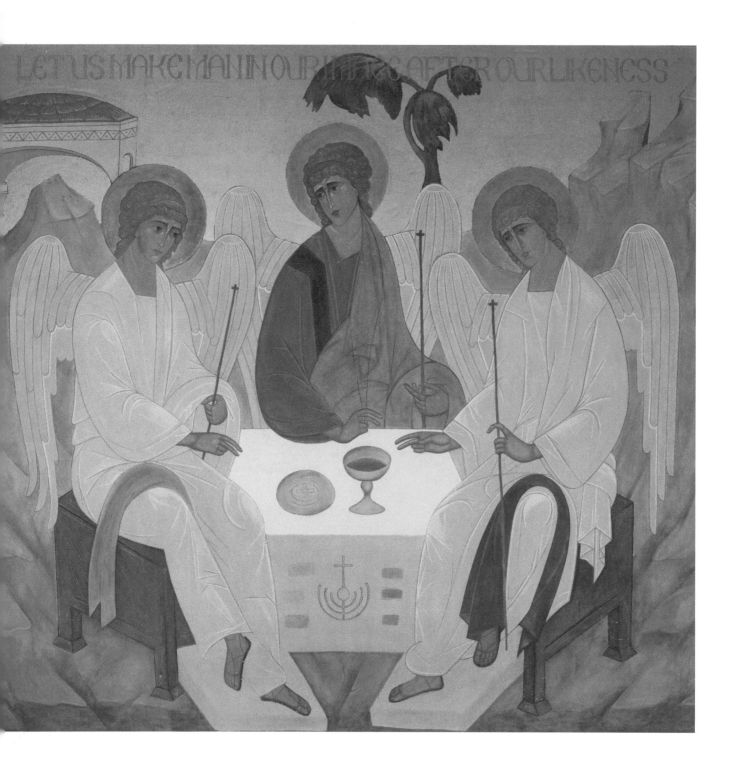

← *Previous page*
Refectory, west view

↑ Trinity, Refectory

→ Trinity, Son

↑ Trinity, Father

→ Trinity, Holy Spirit

ХС   ST·JOHN THE BAPTIST·

← *Previous page* Deisis, Refectory

→ Christ, detail of Deisis

← Crucifixion and
   Resurrection

← The Empty Tomb

← The Angel at the Empty Tomb

← The Myrrh-bearing
Women

↑ The Last Supper, Refectory

↑ Christ, Last Supper

↑ *Top left* St Peter, *top right* St Simon, *bottom left* St James of Alpheus, *bottom right* St Matthew

← *Pages 100-101* Refectory, east view

← *Pages 102-103* St Silouan's Chapel, east view

→ *Pages 105-107* Christ, detail Last Supper

← St John
→ St Simon

↑ *Top left* St James Zebedee, *top right* St Peter, *bottom left* St Andrew, *bottom right* St Matthew

↑ *Top left* St Bartholomew, *top right* St James of Alpheus, *bottom left* St Thaddeus, *bottom right* St Philip

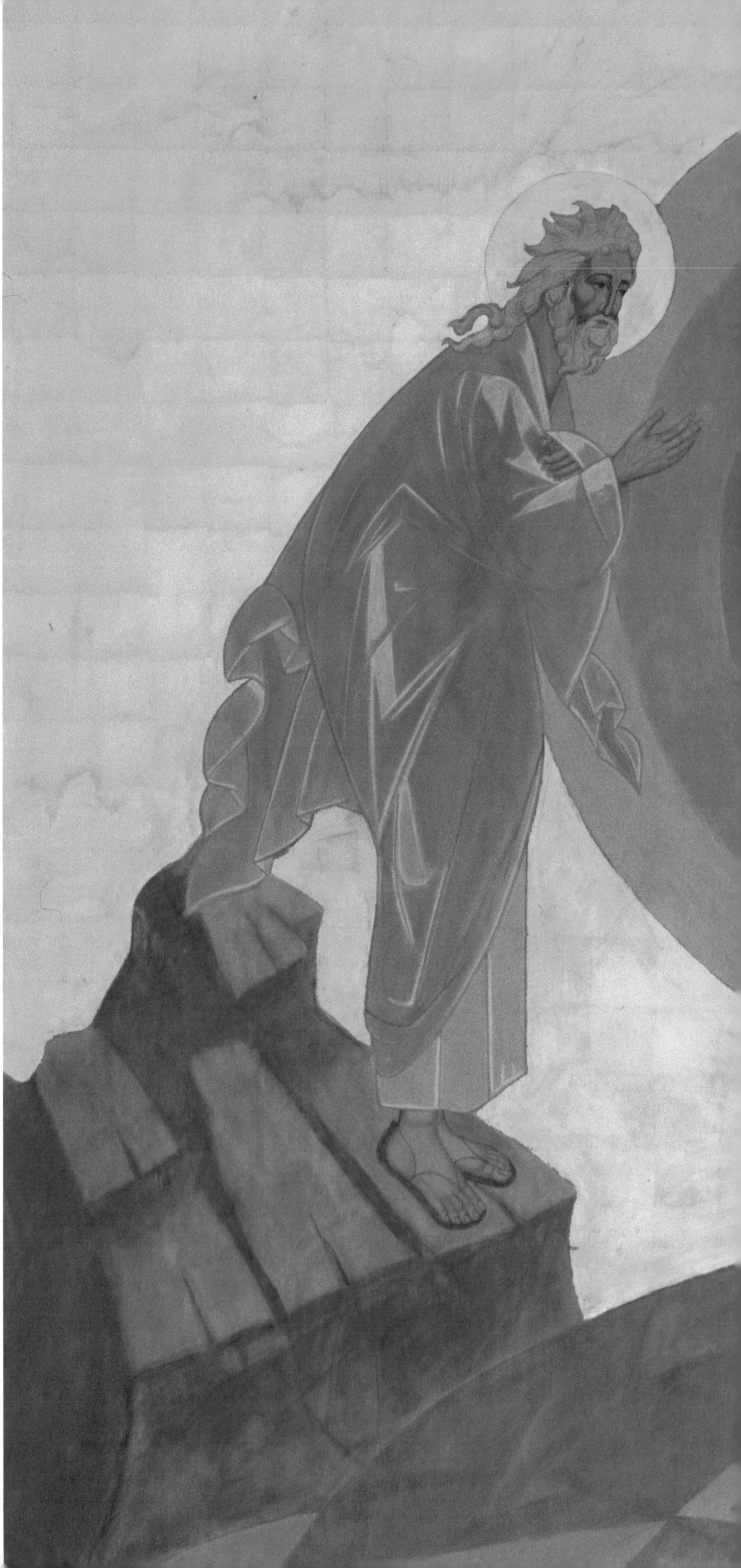

→ The Transfiguration, detail

← Christ,
Crucifixion

← The Resurrection

↑ Adam

↑ Eve

↑ Christ, detail of the Dormition

↑ Mother of God, Ascension

↙ Christt with the soul
of the Mother of God,
Dormition

→ Angel and apostles,
detail of the Ascension

↑ St Matthew, Pentecost

↑ St Paul, Pentecost

↑ Row of Ascetics, St Silouan's Chapel

← St Silouan the Athonite

↑ St Nilus of Sora

↗ St Seraphim of Sarov

PANEL ICONS

Icon painting has a different technical approach from murals as thicker paint is applied in order to obtain a depth of colour, a high quality of surface texture, and a strong presence. The icons reproduced here were painted both for commissions and for the use of the monastery.

For a full commentary on each icon, refer to pages 191 to 192, and for a description of techniques, refer to pages 179 to 182.

↑ St Panteleimon

↑ St Andrew

↑ St Andrew
→ Detail

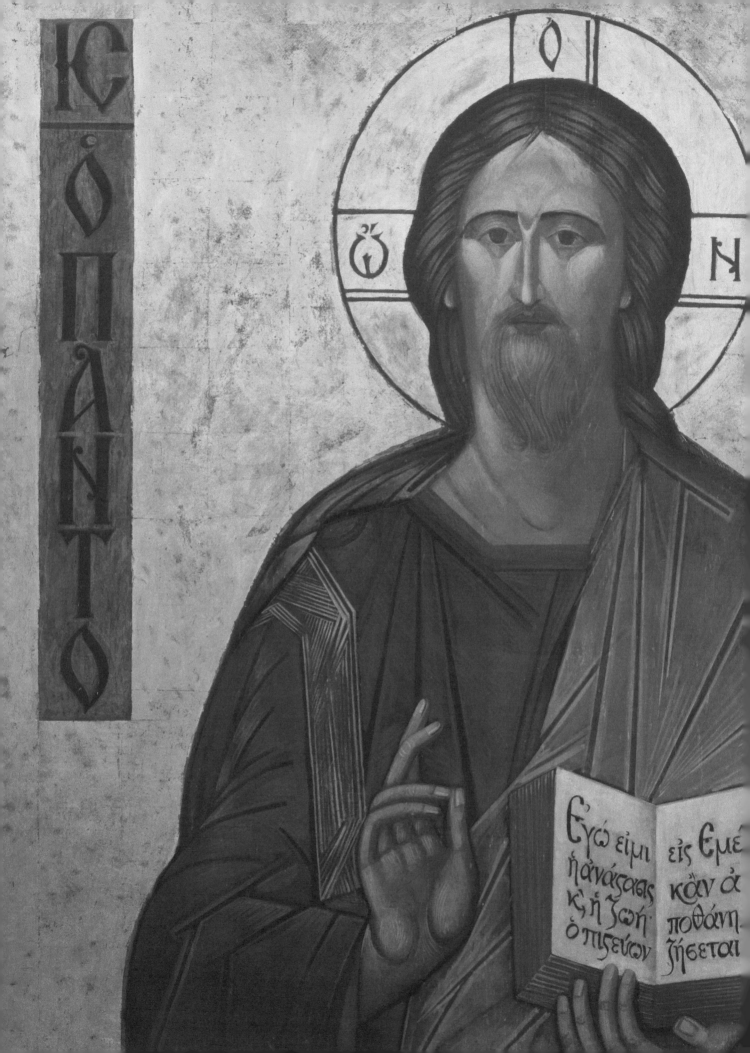

← Christ, All Saints Church

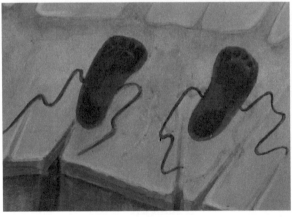 

← Prophet Moses
   receiving the Law

↗ Details

← St Sophrony
   of Jerusalem

→ St Sophrony of
   Jerusalem, detail

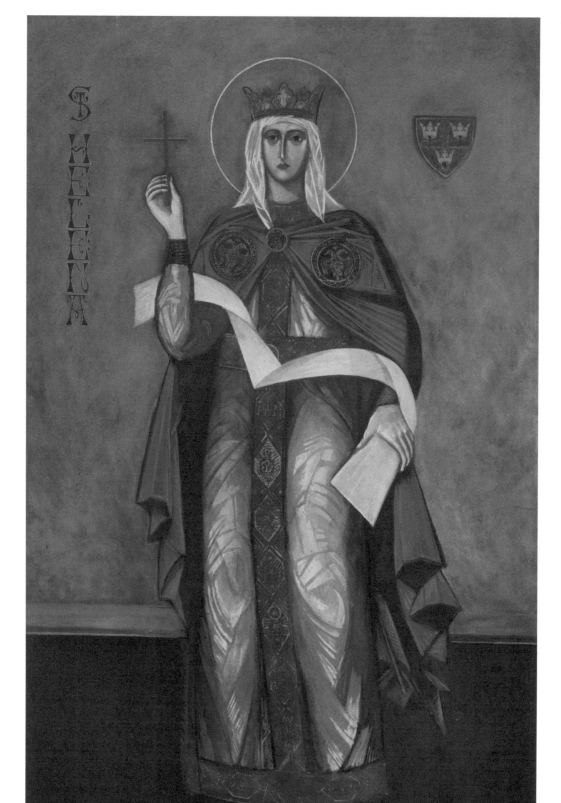

← St Helen

→ St Helen,
 detail

144

← Mother of God

→ Christ in Glory

→ *Pages 150-151*
Details of Christ
in Glory

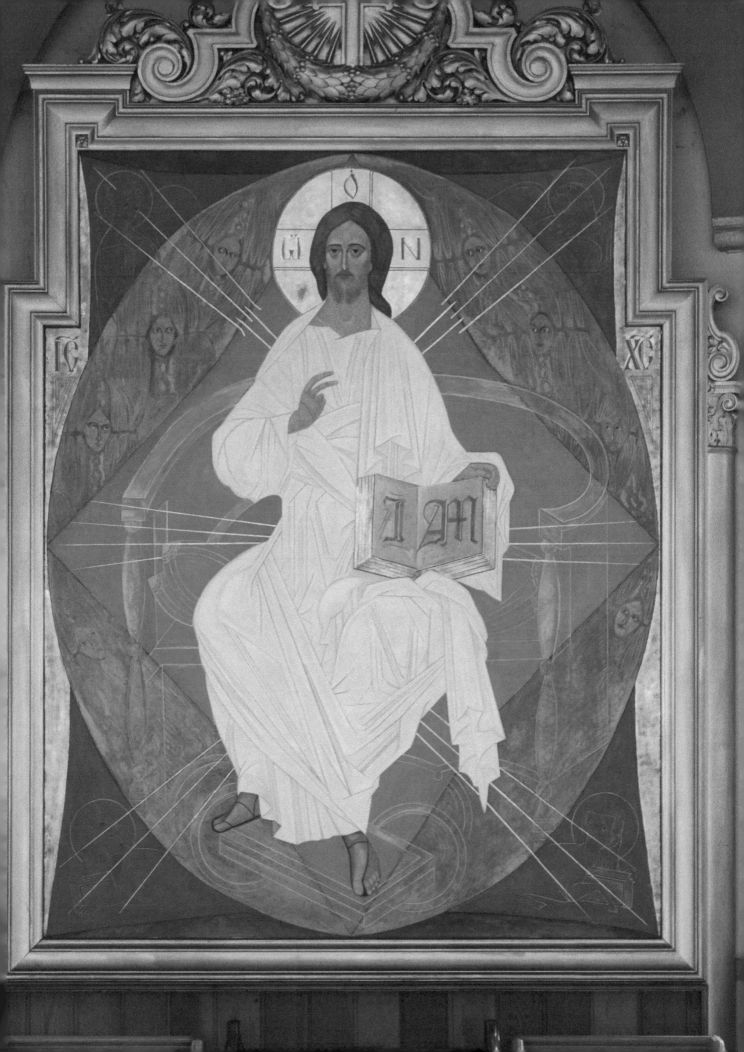

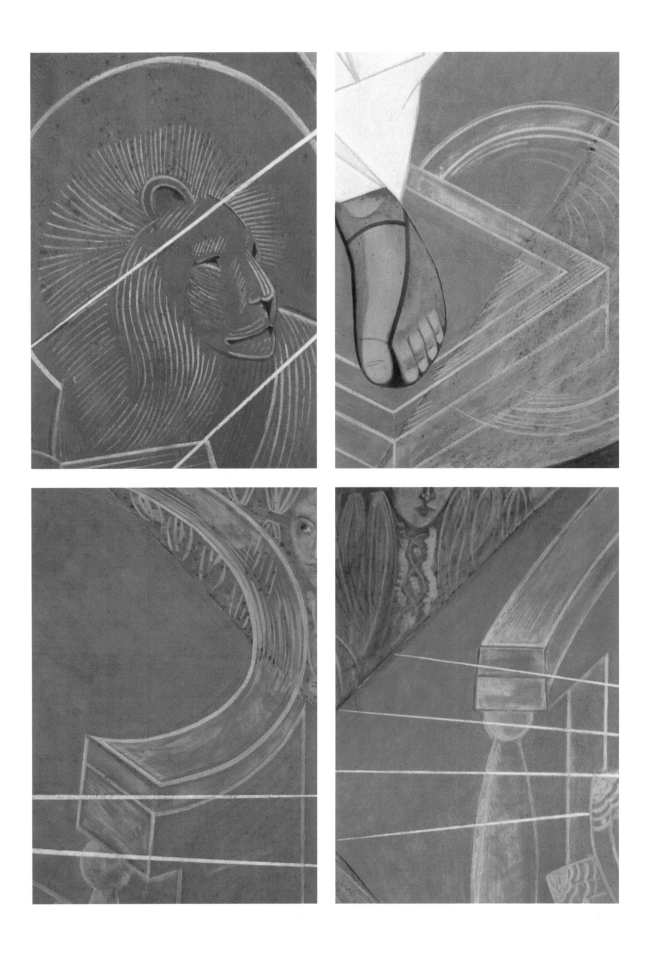

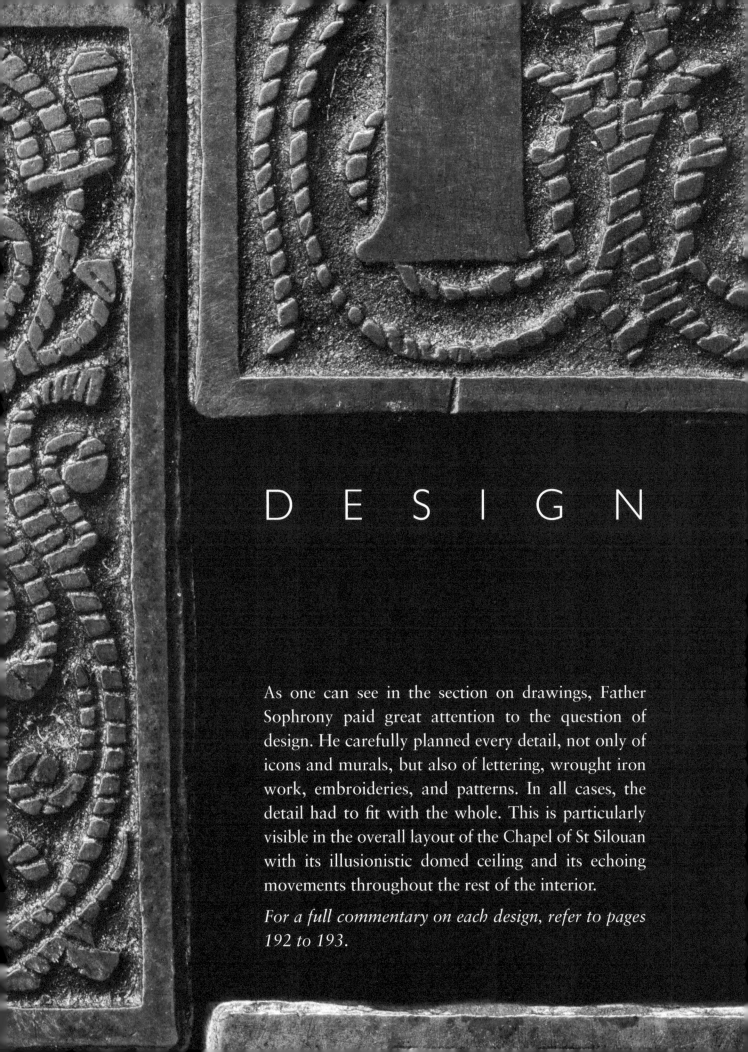

D E S I G N

As one can see in the section on drawings, Father Sophrony paid great attention to the question of design. He carefully planned every detail, not only of icons and murals, but also of lettering, wrought iron work, embroideries, and patterns. In all cases, the detail had to fit with the whole. This is particularly visible in the overall layout of the Chapel of St Silouan with its illusionistic domed ceiling and its echoing movements throughout the rest of the interior.

For a full commentary on each design, refer to pages 192 to 193.

→ Embroidery of St Gabriel

← Embroidery of St Gabriel, reverse side

← Sketch for letters

→ Sketched designs

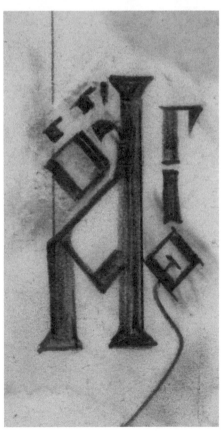

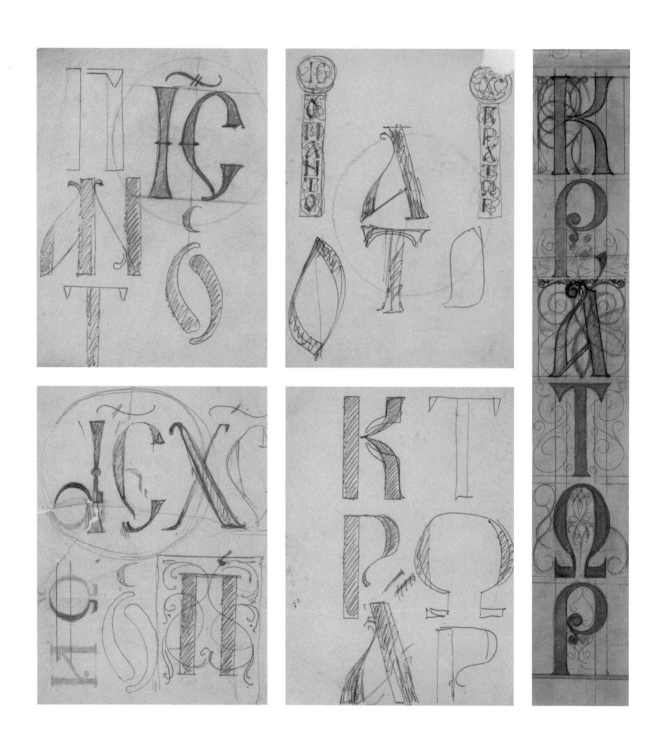

160

← Sketches for letters

↖ Letters from icon of St Helen

↑ Letters from icon of St Andrew

← Metal type letters and decorative elements

→ *Pages 164-167* Metal type letters and printed impression

→ *Pages 168 -169* Metal plate for cover, and printed cover
with hand written inscription

ся
л
с

дня образ м

черной жи

каждый день
и

В нашей б

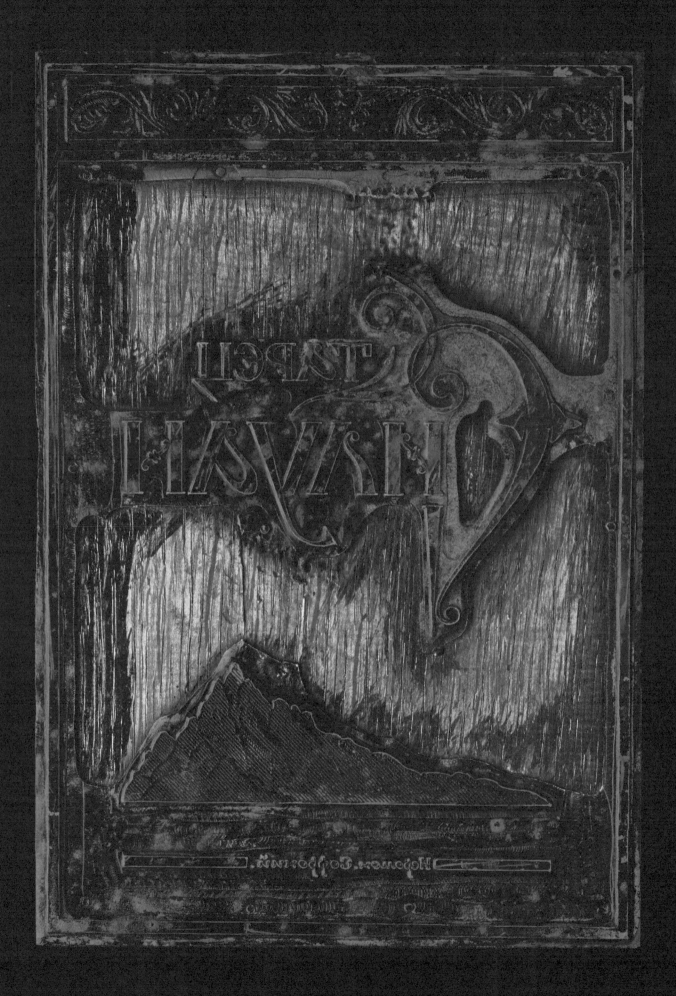

Еще юной Марии
Архимандрит Софроний
со всяким благословением, со многой
молитвой и любовью
6 февраля 1983.

СТАРЕЦ СИЛУАН

"Дух Святой учит нас
смирению Христову,
чтобы душа всегда носила
в себе благодать Божию,
которая веселит
душу"

Ст. Силуан
стр. 161.

Иеромон. Софроний.

Stavropegic Cross,
emblem of the Monastery

← Carpet for Royal Doors,
  St John's Chapel

→ Carpet for Royal Doors,
  St Silouan's Chapel

BIOGRAPHY[1]

Father Sophrony, who was known as Sergei Semeonovich Sakharov before he became a monk, was born in 1896 in Moscow. From an early age he showed artistic talent and as a young man continued to pursue art as a career. He took private lessons in drawing and painting in preparation for the strict entrance exam to the Moscow Institute of Painting, Sculpture and Architecture, the Moscow equivalent of the Academy of Art in Saint Petersburg. His application in 1918 coincided with the institute being reformed to suit the new post-revolutionary state of affairs. He joined what then became known as the "Free State Art Studios" (Svomas) which the following year was changed again into "The Higher State Artistic-Technical Workshops" (VKhUTEMAS). Here he joined the studio of Petr Konchalovsky (1876-1956), a leading artist working in the Russian Cézannesque style. Together with fellow students from the studio, he formed a group called *Bytie* ("Being") which concentrated on plein-air or landscape painting. During the years of his adolescence, he had also been deeply influenced by the writings and works of Kandinsky, seeking pure painting and expression in abstract art.

With time Sergei felt that the atmosphere of the new regime in Russia stifled the possibility of artistic development. In 1922 he and a close artist friend, Leonardo Benatov, decided to emigrate to Paris. They travelled through Italy, staying for a while in Berlin en route. In Paris Sergei soon had the opportunity to exhibit at the *Salon d'Automne* and a year later in the select group of the *Salon des Tuileries*. However, by this time his priorities had changed as he went through intense inner struggles searching for a deeper meaning to life. The outcome of this was that Sergei left his artistic career to engage more completely in a life of prayer. Eventually his search led him to Greece, to the monasteries of Mount Athos, where he became a monk and was given the name, Sophrony. He scarcely painted at all during this period. After living there for 22 years, Father Sophrony returned to France, partly for health reasons and partly to publish the writings of his spiritual director, Staretz Silouan (1866-1938).

In France a small group of followers gathered around him wanting to live a monastic life. Father Sophrony searched for a permanent place for his community to live and finally a disused old rectory was found in the Essex countryside in England. Here he established a monastery which grew beyond his dreams and expectations. It was at this time he took up painting again, now to create icons and murals for use in the monastery.

---

[1] For a fuller account of his life, see: Sister Gabriela, *Seeking Perfection in the World of Art*, Tolleshunt Knights: Stavropegic Monastery of St John the Baptist, 2014;
Sister Gabriela, *'BEING' The Art and Life of Father Sophrony*, Tolleshunt Knights: Stavropegic Monastery of St John the Baptist, 2016.

FATHER SOPHRONY'S TECHNIQUES

Father Sophrony's earliest artistic studies were based on the curriculum of the Academy of Art,[1] copying plaster casts, making figure drawings from models, painting portraits, still lifes, genre paintings, and landscapes. He was also keenly following all the latest developments of both the avant-garde as well as the more traditional older artists. At the post-revolutionary art school he studied the Russian Cézannesque school but was also influenced by all the other modern trends that were represented at the school, from purely abstract art to sculpture and constructivism.

Of all these techniques, he was the most familiar with oil painting. His early works show the use of palette knife application as well as finer brushwork. The portraits he exhibited in the Paris *Salon d'Automne* in 1923[2] were greeted by a prominent art critic[3] who compared them favourably to the work of the sublime French painter Louis-Gustave Ricard (1823-73) in their fine blending and smooth painting. It is significant that his works were not hung with the other Russian painters, but were displayed in a room adjacent to the hall where Cézanne's work was exhibited. During his time in France he earned his living by painting portraits.

When Father Sophrony started to paint icons, he studied the art of egg tempera painting and used this technique. He made a point of sending several of his monks to study with Leonid Ouspensky[4] in Paris in order to learn icon-painting in its traditional form. On several occasions, when faced with technical problems, he consulted this master of iconography. The icons therefore were painted in the traditional manner using earth pigments starting with the darker tones and finishing with the lighter ones on top, producing the effect of light coming from within. Often on large icons, strong undercoats of solid colours were preferred beneath the top shade. This helped to create a vivid presence of the saint or subject painted. The Russian 'floating' style[5] was used when colours were painted on panels in a flat position. In this case, both thicker tones and glazes in a very diluted state were applied or 'floated'. However when an important work had to be finished, Father Sophrony preferred to use oils since he was most familiar with this medium. For this he chose a method which technically did not contradict the traditional iconographic recipe: he covered the egg tempera with its traditional varnish of *olifa*, boiled linseed oil, finally touching up the painting, the face in particular, with artistic oil paints mixed with the same *olifa*.

---

[1] He did not study at the Academy, but at private studios based on the curriculum of the Academy. Several sources state the contrary, but recent examination of the archives of the Academy confirms that he was not enrolled there.

[2] The two paintings he exhibited were *Head of a woman* and *Portrait of a man*. See catalogue of Salon d'Automne 1923, entries 1792 and 1793, page 279.

[3] Thiebault-Sisson writing in *Le Temps*, 31.10.1923.

[4] Leonid Ouspensky (1902-1987) was one of the main revivers of iconography in the Paris emigration.

[5] As opposed to the Greek technique of painting upright with undiluted colours.

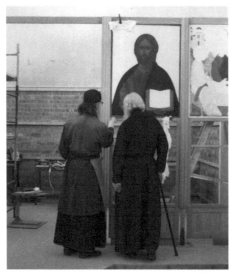

All images Father Sophrony working in St Silouan's Chapel

↑ *Lower left* Father Sophrony working in the Refectory

This allowed him to use thin transparent glazes which blended and united with the lower layers of the varnished egg tempera. With time this technique proved to be so useful that icons were deliberately left with just under-painting, often done by an assistant. After the first varnish, Father Sophrony would continue to render the face applying the finishing touches. Finally the whole icon would receive another layer of *olifa* to keep a united and continuous surface, preferably resembling porcelain or ivory.

The culture of the surface was of great importance to Father Sophrony, especially in the case of wall paintings. Here it was of prime importance that the surface be totally matt or non-reflective, while the painting was to be light and luminous in order to produce walls with paintings that would not impose themselves but form a suitable atmosphere and space for prayer. He reasoned that the church, where monks spent most days and nights, was their 'living room'. As such the walls should be in harmony with the Liturgy in particular and not be disturbing or tiring for those present. In addition, the colour of the walls and the lighting of the room had to be considered. These were difficult decisions which required much time in order to find the best method for painting the murals. Finally it was decided to paint straight on to the normal gypsum plaster, after first sanding off the troweled top surface which was hard and non-absorbent. Once this layer was removed, the walls became absorbent and a combination of artistic oil-paint heavily diluted in turpentine was chosen. The thin paint penetrated the walls which stayed totally matt provided the coats were not too rich in oil, giving a final effect not dissimilar to that of real fresco. For blocking in the colour and for shading and gradation, the paint was applied with cloths folded as pads. Later, Father Sophrony added lines and features modeling the faces with delicate shades and glazes which he applied by brush. In order to avoid the use of white paint which can give a heavy effect, the highlights on the faces, garments, and mountains were achieved by lightly scratching or sandpapering the surface to expose the gentle white shade of the gypsum plaster. The details and finer qualities of the works are not generally visible in situ, which is why several large-scale fragments have been reproduced in this book.

Before commencing work on a face, Father Sophrony made several preparatory drawings, first as studies and finally as exact drawings of the facial features. Another consideration was the scale, size, and position of each figure. Certain apostles appear repeatedly in several murals. The most studied and carefully painted faces are in the two scenes of the Last Supper,[6] and it was for these that the preparatory drawings were done. As the apostles appear smaller in some other scenes, the rendering becomes different: the principle traits are still the same, but the way the painting is executed becomes less refined. Attention is given to the basic characteristics and not so much to detail. Some of these examples have been included in this book as a comparative study.

The post-revolutionary influence on Father Sophrony can be seen in his compositions where an underlying constructivist aspect is present. These scenes have leading lines and forms which create movements that follow through the painted figures, garments, mountains, and objects. Ideally, each part of the mural should be linked with its surroundings by an echoed line, a followed movement or

---

[6] The Last Supper was painted both in the Refectory and in the Chapel, each time following the same basic lay-out, but with great difference in the treatment of the faces: in the Refectory the painting was stronger and bolder, while in the Chapel the faces were more modeled with gentler tones and hues.

paint stroke. These underlying structures give a strength which is often invisible except for a trained eye. For large scale drawings, Father Sophrony used pre-cut shapes in hardboard. These facilitated the repetition and unity of line and composition. Often the same line and shape were used without being seen or felt as a repetition, yet the eye would feel calm from the harmony produced. These were used especially for the ceiling angels in the Refectory, the first large mural project.

Father Sophrony also made preparatory studies in soft pastel. With this method he was able to test the colouring and expression in a more palpable way than that of shaded pencil drawings. This was particularly important in the case of the large icon of Christ in Glory painted in the early 1970s.[7] This icon was so large that in order to use the floating egg tempera technique, it was necessary to paint the face from the top of the panel, in effect 'upside down'. In this case a pastel study proved to be essential, as it was otherwise impossible to judge the expression.

Father Sophrony's decorative work is best illustrated by the typography he created for the first printed edition of his book *Staretz Silouan* in Russian.[8] He designed and probably carved or etched the letter blocks himself. Here one can see traces of the pre-revolutionary Russian book tradition, rich in ornament and embellishments, while at the same time keeping a strict and sober style more suggestive of the later post-revolutionary designs.

As for the inscriptions on icons, Father Sophrony was concerned that the lettering be decorative and not too legible. He reasoned that in modern life one is bombarded with texts which may be read automatically without much attention, while if a text demands a slight effort to decipher, one is more likely to remember it.

Generally Father Sophrony paid great attention to design and detail, both for individual objects as well as for general settings like the colours and tones of adjacent buildings and the lay-out and planning of gardens. The most spectacular illustration of this is the interior of St Silouan's Chapel. Due to building restrictions, it was not possible to construct the desired roof structure, so Father Sophrony created an interior design of a virtual dome by the use of concentric circles, gold, bronze and large superimposed Seraphim angels. The dynamics of this design were repeated in the tapestry of the altar carpet and reflected in lines within the wall paintings, achieving a unity which is not obvious, but which is felt in an overall sense of harmony.

---

[7] For illustration of the icon, see page 149.

[8] Printed 1952 in Paris.

Notes on illustrations*

Page	Comments

18/19 *Middle Angel, the "Son"*, mid/late 1970s, from *The Holy Trinity*.
See notes for page 29.

21 *Christ*, 1972, pastel on paper, 50 x 34.5cm. Preparatory study for icon *Christ in Glory*. Welling, Church of St Michael.

Father Sophrony's fascination with the face of Christ remained with him all his life and he continued to work right into his old age trying to portray it evermore faithfully.

"There is no icon of Christ that corresponds to our thoughts, expectations and dreams. When I see an icon of Christ, I just note that it IS Christ and my mind soars up immeasurably higher."

The icon for the church in Welling was so large (213.3 x 152.4 cm) that in order to use the Russian floating technique where the panel has to be kept horizontal, the face had to be painted from the top of the panel, upside down, therefore it was essential to have an exact study to work from, as it is impossible to control the expression and fine detail of the face when not in front of it.

For the finished icon, see page 149.

22 *Christ*, mid/late 1970s, pencil on greaseproof paper, 44.3 x 38.2 cm. Drawing for mural of *The Resurrection*. Community of St John the Baptist, Refectory.

The drawings for the murals were done in preparation for the final work, mapping out areas of shade and the dividing lines in a somewhat stylized manner. The priority in this drawing was to find the expression of Christ looking at Adam, His first formed man, as He drew him up out of hell.

For the finished painting, see page 89.

23 *Christ*, mid/late 1970s, pencil on tracing paper, 38.5 x 41.5 cm. Drawing for the *Deisis* mural, Refectory.

Deisis is a composition where Christ is in the centre and on each side of Him are saints in an attitude of reverence and prayer.

This drawing concentrates on the positioning of the features while their actual expression was left until the painting stage.

See notes below for page 84/85.

For the finished mural see pages 84–85 and 87.

24 *Christ*, 1972, pencil on tracing paper, 60.7 x 48.8 cm. Preliminary sketch for icon of *Christ in Glory* (see note for page 21).

Often several preliminary sketches were made to find the exact representation needed.

See page 21 for finished study and page 149 for finished icon.

25 *Christ*, 1988, pencil on discoloured greaseproof paper, 39 x 31.3 cm. Drawing for icon on *iconostasis*, St Silouan's Chapel, Community of St John the Baptist.

As mentioned above, Father Sophrony never ceased in his attempt to portray the Face of Christ more faithfully. Every time, at best only a small fragment came near to what he sought.

26 *Left Angel, the "Father"*, mid/late 70s, pastel on paper, 55.7 x 37 cm. Colour study for *The Holy Trinity* mural, Refectory.

As this face was of particular importance, Father Sophrony made an exact pastel study to find the expression needed before starting work on the wall. The nature of the walls was such that they were easily saturated, therefore only a small amount of paint could be used in order to avoid an unwanted sheen. For this reason the preparatory drawings had to be thoroughly worked out so the changes needed on the wall were kept to a minimum and a matt surface could be preserved.

For finished mural, see pages 80 and 82.

27 *Left Angel, the "Father"*, mid/late 70s, pencil on greaseproof paper, 48.5 x 34.3 cm. Drawing for *The Holy Trinity* mural, Refectory.
See notes for page 26.

28 *Angel*, mid/late 70s, pencil on newsprint, 50.7 x 38.3 cm. Drawing for angel at *The Empty Tomb*, Refectory.

In this drawing full attention has been given to the features, while the shading has been schematically mapped out with delineating lines and hatching.

For finished mural, see pages 90 and 92.

29 *Middle Angel, the "Son"*, mid/late 1970s, pencil and pen on paper, 55.9 x 43.2 cm. Drawing for *The Holy Trinity*, Refectory.

Several drawings were done to find the exact expression in the most minimalistic and direct manner.

See pages 80 and 81.

30 *Angel, symbol of St Matthew*, 1972, pencil and pen on paper, 51 x 46.5 cm. Sketch for icon *Christ in Glory*.

This drawing already indicates what is intended at the painting stage by using colour for some of the lines, mapping out the exact positioning on the panel. Note the dynamics of this figure with repeated semicircular lines which reflect the direction of the gaze.

For finished icon, see page 149, top left hand corner.

31 *Eagle, symbol of St John*, 1972, pencil on paper, 47.4 x 57 cm. Drawing for icon *Christ in Glory*.

This drawing shows how the figure was worked with

---

* All the measurements given, indicate first the height of left side, followed by the width of top edge.
All works reproduced here are from private collections, unless otherwise stated.
All quotes in italic are comments of Father Sophrony, sourced from the author's notes.

the trial lines and erased shapes still visible. The paper was then turned over to use the reverse of the image as seen in the following illustration.

32 *Eagle, symbol of St John*, 1972, coloured pencil on paper, 31 x 57 cm. Drawing for icon *Christ in Glory*. Reverse side of drawing on page 31, paper not symmetrical.

Here the main lines visible from the other side of the drawing were overlaid in red and were then transferred to the panel.

For finished icon, see page 149, top right hand corner.

33 *Lion, symbol of Saint Mark*, 1972, pen on paper (envelope), 22 x 21.5 cm. Sketch for icon of *Christ in Glory*.

Often ideas were 'tried out' on whatever paper was at hand, in this case an envelope, typifying the phrase, "back-of-the-envelope-calculation", a traditional way of testing thoughts, theories and ideas.

For finished painting, see page 149, bottom left corner, for close up, see page 150 top left image.

34 *Seraphim Angel*, 1972, pencil on paper, 59 x 48.5 cm. Sketch for icon of *Christ in Glory*.

Christ seated on His throne of glory is surrounded by the heavenly hosts, symbolized by Seraphim angels in blue. They are "all eyes", so the expression sought was one of attentive tension. This is the first attempt to find a type for the face and a schematic shape of the wings.

See page 149 for full icon and pages 150/151 for fragments of other Seraphim angels.

35 *Seraphim Angel*, mid 1970s, watercolour on paper, 59.6 x 50.6 cm. Study for ceiling of Refectory.

Several trials were made to find how to represent the ceiling angels in the Refectory. As, *"Angels are fire"*, attempts were made to represent this with the colour red, but finally a normal iconographic skin colour of yellow ochre was chosen.

36 *Seraphim Angel*, early 1980s, pencil on greaseproof paper, 38 x 44.7 cm. Preliminary sketch for ceiling, St Silouan's Chapel.

As mentioned earlier (see note for page 34), Seraphim angels are "all eyes" and trials were made as to how this could be represented.

"They don't have any gesture, they just LOOK."

"The Seraphims can be severe, to evoke a salutary fear in the onlooker."

37 *Red Seraphim Angel*, early 1980s, pastel on paper, 56 x 32 cm. Study of face for ceiling in St Silouan's Chapel.

"The Seraphim above the altar looks down at the Holy Table.

The Seraphims should look like Christ, having similar features such as hair etc, as they are created in His Image and have the same age as Him."

38/39 *The Annunciation*, mid/late 1960s, pencil on paper, 57 x 93 cm. Drawing for *The Royal Doors*, iconostasis, parish of St Nicholas, Southampton.

Note the dynamic lines of movement combined with a minimalistic drawing of the figures and the circular shapes throughout the composition.

40/41 *Hands of Christ*, early/mid 1980s, pencil on greaseproof paper, right hand (page 40) 22.8 x 37.8 cm, left hand (page 41) 21 x 34 cm. Drawings for *The Last Supper*, St Silouan's Chapel.

"It is important to have harmony, nothing discordant or unbalanced, yet at the same time, there should be no repetition in the details, no mirrored hand or eye."

42 *Hand of Mother of God at the Cross*, early/mid 80s, pencil on paper, 15.7 x 27.5 cm. Drawing for mural of *The Crucifixion*, St Silouan's Chapel. Signed AS (Archimandrite Sophrony).

43 *Hand of Apostle Philip*, early/mid 1980s, pencil on greaseproof paper, 37.8 x 27.5 cm. Drawing for *Last Supper*, St Silouan's Chapel.

Father Sophrony gave the following guideline for drawing hands:

"You have to follow the hand's anatomical measurements but then adopt throughout some special 'style' even if you copy from different sources."

44 *Legs and feet of Prophet Moses*, 1985, pencil on greaseproof paper, 24.2 x 17.7 cm. Drawing for icon *Prophet Moses Receiving the Law*, signed AS.

Note the economy of line, giving direction and full movement in a minimalistic manner.

For finished icon, see pages 138/139.

45 *Prophet Moses Receiving the Law, detail*, 1985, pencil and egg tempera on greaseproof paper, 65.6 x 37.2 cm. Drawing for icon *Prophet Moses Receiving the Law*.

Here Father Sophrony worked over a drawing made by an assistant, emphasizing and developing it. Yellow ochre paint was added to underline the construction and expression of the face.

For finished icon see pages 138/139.

46 *Mother of God at the Cross*, early/mid 80s, pencil on greaseproof paper, 47 x 38 cm. Drawing for mural of *The Crucifixion*, St Silouan's Chapel.

This is another example of a preliminary drawing by an assistant being worked over by Father Sophrony. Attention has been mainly given to the face, but some bolder lines may be seen in the outline and folds which correcting the shape, then connects more directly with the expression of the face.

47 *Christ crucified*, early/mid 80s, pencil on greaseproof paper, 40 x 33 cm. Drawing for mural of *The Crucifixion*, St Silouan's Chapel.

This drawing is worked entirely by Father Sophrony. Because of the importance of the subject it is given the utmost attention and treated as a work in itself, which may be seen in the careful shading, done in a way that already resembles painting.

For finished painting, see pages 115/116.

48   *St John at the Cross*, early/mid 80s, pencil and felt-tip on greaseproof paper, 38 x 28.5 cm. Drawing for mural of *The Crucifixion*, St Silouan's Chapel.

This drawing is worked on top of a tracing of an earlier painting of the same apostle, keeping the features, but changing the expression. The felt tip lines indicate how it is to be positioned on the wall.

Compare with St John at the Last Supper, page 108.

49   *Chinese Saint*, 1959, pen on paper, 21 x 13.4 cm. Impromptu sketch of, *"How a Chinese Saint would look"*, drawn on the back of a letter.

50   *Saint Paissius*, early/mid 1980s, pencil on greaseproof paper, 50.7 x 38 cm. Drawing for the ascetics on the face of the balcony, St Silouan's Chapel.

Note how the scheme for mapping out the face is almost cubist in style. This drawing also illustrates the previous comment that the two sides of the face should not be a mirror image but rather complement each other, so that together they express the person depicted (see note at pages 40/41).

For full row of ascetics, see page 127.

51   *Saint Arsenius*, early/mid 80s, pencil on greaseproof paper, 52.5 x 36.8 cm. Drawing for the ascetics on the face of the balcony, St Silouan's Chapel.

This face has been worked over a preliminary drawing by an assistant and follows the same pattern of construction as the previous one, yet the expression and message conveyed is quite different.

"When drawing the eyes, if a line is drawn across the base to close it a little, the look is intensified, more concentrated and directs the gaze further."

For full wall painting, see page 127.

52   *Adam*, early/mid 80s, pencil on greaseproof paper, 48 x 38 cm. Drawing for mural of *The Resurrection*, Refectory and St Silouan's Chapel.

This is a tracing of the face of Adam in the Refectory, with the stronger pencil lines indicating how Father Sophrony altered the drawing slightly when transferring it onto the wall of the Chapel. As the face in the Refectory was developed on the wall, a tracing was made of it from which to work for the depiction of Adam in the Chapel.

See pages 89 and 118 for finished paintings.

53   *Eve,* early/mid 80s, pencil on greaseproof paper, 42 x 38 cm. Drawing for mural of *The Resurrection*, Refectory and St Silouan's Chapel. See notes above. Tracing not done by Father Sophrony.

See pages 89 and 119.

55   *St Helen*, 1960s, pencil on paper, 25.4 x 20.4 cm. Drawing for icon *St Helen of Colchester*.

The drawing for St Helen's face was developed on this side of the paper and then turned over, see note for page 56.

See page 144.

56   *St Helen*, 1960s, pencil on paper, 25.4 x 20.4 cm.

Another example of using the reverse side of a drawing for the finished work, see *Eagle* for the icon of *Christ in Glory*, see notes for pages 31 and 32.

The drawing depicted on the previous page was positioned face down on the panel with a pigment transfer-paper in between and only the lines of the main features were repeated and transferred to the icon panel.

See finished face on page 145.

57   *St Andrew*, 1960s, coloured pen on paper, 27.1 x 21 cm. Sketch to make an exploratory study of the saint, not intended for an icon.

Note the freedom in the lines and movements throughout the figure. The use of pen directly without any underlying pencil drawing and as such not giving the possibility for correction shows a sure hand and clear thought.

58   *St Naum of Ohrid,* 1960s, pencil on paper, 30 x 21 cm. This is an example of a more strictly iconographic drawing, without any personal interpretation.

59   *St Sophrony of Jerusalem*, 1970s, pencil on paper, 55.2 x 24.2 cm. Detail of drawing for icon of *St Sophrony of Jerusalem*.

Several drawings were made to portray Father Sophrony's own patron saint. His aim was to give an eagle-like gaze, fitting for a bishop, with the eyes slightly apart, to give an all-encompassing, far-reaching look.

For finished icon, see pages 140 and 141.

60   *St Silouan the Athonite*, early/mid 1980s, pencil on grease-proof paper, 54.2 x 37 cm. Drawing for ascetics on face of balcony, St Silouan's Chapel.

This is the first frontal image of St Silouan made by Father Sophrony. He used his techniques in portrait drawing to capture the likeness. As an icon is primarily a spiritual portrait to convey the inner image of the person, while at the same time preserving their recognizable physical features, Father Sophrony only partly drew upon photographs of his elder. He described how Saint Silouan's facial expressions were constantly changing, as is common with praying people and could not be conveyed by photography.

For finished mural, see pages 127 and 128.

61   *St Silouan the Athonite*, mid/late 1970s, pencil on tracing paper, 64.5 x 39.2 cm. Drawing for mural i n Refectory.

This drawing by Father Sophrony was based on the first icon painted of St Silouan by Leonid Ouspensky in the 1950s in Paris. Emphasis is given to the look of the saint, in supplication to Christ, depicted in the top corner of the mural.

62   *St Zacharias*, 1960s, pen on paper, 25.3 x 20.2 cm. Drawing for an icon.

Here the aim was to portray a prophet, a Biblical figure, giving an expression of wisdom and timelessness.

63   *St Zacharias*, 1960s, pen on paper, 39.4 x 32.5 cm. Drawing for same icon, as page 62.

64   *St James of Zebedee*, mid/late 1970s, pencil on paper, 33.8 x 28 cm. Drawing for *The Last Supper*, Refectory.

This was one of the preliminary studies for the apostles, searching for the way to express how they listened to Christ with reverence and attention.

For finished mural see page 96, fourth apostle from the left.

65   *St Matthew*, mid/late 1970s, pencil on greaseproof paper with grid, 44.3 x 34 cm. Drawing for *The Last Supper*, Refectory, also used in St Silouan's Chapel.

The grid was used as a method of enlarging the drawing to the scale needed. The enlarging would be done by an assistant and then the drawing would again be touched up by Father Sophrony. In this case it is a drawing that has already been enlarged to the right dimension, and then drawn over again by Father Sophrony, as can be seen by the erased squares within the figure.

For finished paintings see pages 99 and 110.

66   *St Thaddeus*, mid/late 1970s, pencil on greaseproof paper with grid, 35.5 x 28 cm. Drawing for *The Last Supper*, Refectory.

As in the case of page 64, this was a preliminary study, trying to capture the features and character of the apostle. The finished painting evolved further, as can be seen on the whole scene, page 96, second apostle from left.

68   *St Bartholomew*, mid/late 1970s, pencil on greaseproof paper with blue grid, 49.4 x 37.2 cm. Drawing for *The Last Supper*, Refectory.

Here is an example of an enlarged drawing with only the most important lines redrawn by Father Sophrony.

The final image of this apostle evolved during the painting, see page 96, third apostle from the left.

69   *St Peter*, mid/late 1970s, pencil on paper, 36.4 x 31 cm. Drawing for *The Last Supper*, Refectory.

For finished mural see page 99, St Peter is on the top left hand. His image evolved throughout the work.

70   *St Paul*, early/mid 1980s, pencil on greaseproof paper, 38 x 25.7 cm. Drawing for *Ascension* and *Pentecost*, St Silouan's Chapel.

The model taken for this drawing was Rublev's famous icon of St Paul. The same drawing was used in the two scenes of feasts in which St Paul appears, but the head positioned at different angles.

See pages 123 and 125 for the final paintings.

71   *St James of Alpheus*, mid/late 1970s, pencil on paper with grid, 50 x 35 cm. Drawing for *The Last Supper*, Refectory.

Enlarged drawing on top of a grid, with the main lines redrawn by Father Sophrony in slightly different directions than the enlargement.

For finished mural, see page 97 (second from right), page 99 (lower left) and for a later version, page 111.

72   *St Bartholomew*, mid/late 1970s, pencil on greaseproof paper with red grid, 37.2 x 27.2 cm. Drawing for *The Last Supper*, Refectory.

This is an original drawing, compare with enlarged drawing on page 68.

73   *St James of Zebedee*, early/mid 1980s, pencil on greaseproof paper, 41.2 x 30 cm. Drawing for *The Last Supper*, St Silouan's Chapel.

A fresh drawing was made of this apostle for the Last Supper in the Chapel.

See page 110, top left.

74   *St Thomas*, mid/late 1970s, pencil on paper with grid, 34.7 x 25.2 cm. Original size drawing for *The Last Supper*, Refectory. The same drawing was also used for the same scene in St Silouan's Chapel.

"St Thomas gave the most profound and all-embracing theological definition, 'My Lord and my God'. I like him very much for that."

See page 96, far left.

75   *St Philip*, mid/late 1970s, pencil on paper with grid, 42 x 36.2 cm. Original portrait drawing as a study for Apostle Philip.

See page 97 far right and page 111 lower right.

76/77   *St John the Baptist,* 1984, oil paint on gypsum plaster. Detail from mural of *The Baptism of Christ*, St Silouan's Chapel.

Emphasis was given to St John bowing in reverence and humility towards Christ whom he is baptizing. The same drawing for the face of St John was used as for *The Deisis*, page 85.

78–101   The Refectory Mural was painted mid/end 1970s–1982, with Father Sophrony taking an active part. The final touches were added 1990–91 under the direction of Father Sophrony.

78/79   General view of the Refectory, west side.

80   *The Holy Trinity*, oil paint on gypsum plaster, 2.94 x 3.58 m. Mural, Refectory.

The model used was based on Rublev's famous icon, but to emphasize that only the second person of the Trinity, Christ, was incarnate, the other two angels were left in white, to give a more incorporeal image.

"The Holy Trinity: A Meeting in Eternity. *They are speaking about the creation. The chalice represents the fallen world's salvation. Christ is the middle angel."*

"This is not a real icon, because only Christ is incarnate, but we recognize the Holy Trinity in this formula."

81   *Middle Angel, the "Son"*, oil paint on gypsum plaster. Detail of *The Holy Trinity*, Mural, Refectory.

This face expresses both love and sorrow over the coming tragedy of the fall of mankind. The icon is an image of the Pre-Eternal Council where the Trinity discuss the risk inherent in creating man free, allowing the possibility of his fall, whereupon the middle Angel, the Son, responds, "In that case I will go and save them."

For preparatory drawings see page 29 and cover image.

82   *Left Angel, the "Father"*, oil paint on gypsum plaster. Detail of *The Holy Trinity*, Mural, Refectory.

This angel looks at both the other two at the same time. His eyes are slightly spaced apart to encompass them both.

For preparatory drawings see page 27 and colour study page 26.

83   *Right Angel, the "Holy Spirit"*, oil paint on gypsum plaster. Detail of *The Holy Trinity*, Mural, Refectory.

"Beauty is achieved when the colour is consistent over the whole face, rather than a bit of yellow or pink etc. here and there."

Father Sophrony thought that yellow ochre was the most noble and fitting colour for faces, in this case with a minimalistic modeling on top. Here is emphasized the expression of humble love and assent.

84/85   *The Deisis*, oil paint on gypsum plaster 2.94 x 3.58 m. Mural, Refectory.

As described previously (see note for page 23), *the Deisis* is the iconographic formula of having Christ in the centre with saints on either side of Him in an attitude of reverence and supplication. The most usual is to have His Mother and St John the Baptist on His right and left respectively. They being foremost among the saints.

87   *Christ*, oil paint on gypsum plaster. Detail of *The Deisis*, Mural, Refectory.

"Christ may be given an all encompassing look by directing the gaze of each eye fractionally apart. From close up they appear slightly disjointed, but from a distance, they look straight. To have the effect that He sees you wherever you are, one can attain it without the above, because the surface is flat, he can look everywhere (in contrast to a sculpture)."

"We must not put many shadows on the face of Christ, He is all light."

For the drawing of this face, see page 23.

88/89   *Crucifixion and Resurrection*, oil paint on gypsum plaster, 2.94 x 3.58 m. Mural, Refectory.

Crucifixion: face painted by a pupil of Father Sophrony, copied from drawing on page 47 and from finished mural page 115.

Resurrection: For drawings of faces see pages 22, 52 and 53.

Father Sophrony intended to make a strong and clear statement in the composition of these two adjacent scenes, emphasizing their difference in the stark contrast of background colour.

"On the icon of the resurrection Adam looks at his Creator with astonishment, Eve also, but not so much, she is a bit troubled. But we will all be astonished on that day."

90/91   *The Empty Tomb*, oil paint on gypsum plaster, 2.94 x 3.58 m. Mural, Refectory.

92/93   *Angel at The Empty Tomb*, oil paint on gypsum plaster. Mural, Refectory.

The face of the Angel is intentionally painted without highlights, as the time of the scene depicted happened at dawn, in twilight.

For full scene see pages 90/92, for drawing, see page 28.

94/95   *Myrrh-bearing Women*, oil paint on gypsum plaster. Mural, Refectory. For full scene see pages 90/91.

96/97   *The Last Supper*, oil paint on gypsum plaster., 2.94 x 7.24 m. Mural, Refectory.

The moment depicted is when Judas left which gave Christ the freedom to speak openly with his disciples. All attention of the apostles is directed towards Christ, drawing the spectator into the mural, emphasized further through the graphic design of reverse perspective on the table.

98   *Christ*, oil paint on gypsum plaster. Detail of *Last Supper* mural, Refectory.

In 1990 Father Sophrony asked one of his assistants to add a little emphasis on Christ's face: *"Make some shadows on the face of Christ, around the nose, under eyebrows, on cheeks, nose etc. But **pray** beforehand because the aim should be that people looking at the Face of Christ will want to correct themselves and every wrong mark will show up and be like a hindrance to them."*

For full scene see pages 96/97.

99   *Apostles*, oil paint on gypsum plaster. Details of *Last Supper* mural, Refectory.

"I would like to give expression in the eyes, in the look…"

Top left: *St Peter*. Compare with preliminary drawing page 69.

Top right: *St Simon*.

Bottom left: *St James of Alpheus*. Compare with early drawing page 71.

Bottom right: *St Matthew*. See drawing page 65.

100/101   Refectory, general view, looking east.

The Refectory was initially planned to be used as a combined Chapel and Refectory. The eastern section with the Last Supper was intended as the sanctuary space. The room was divided into three sections with large curtains from the beams.

102–123   **The St Silouan's Chapel Mural was started in 1983 with work going on until the consecration in 1988.**

102/103   St Silouan's Chapel, east view.

"The Liturgy may be celebrated anywhere, even using a tea bowl and a plate, but if there is a possibility to do better, why not try to strive as perfectly as possible. The Liturgy is not 'a piece of news' to be consumed and disposed of by the evening, nor is it simply the commemoration of an historical event, but it is an eternal reality. That is why we paint 'the Mystical Supper' with only the chalice and the bread on the table."

Work on the Refectory murals was postponed when it became possible to build St Silouan's Chapel. Some of the layout from the Refectory was repeated in the Chapel, especially *The Last Supper*, with minor alterations.

105   *Christ*, mid 1980s, oil paint on gypsum plaster. Detail of *The Last Supper*, St Silouan's Chapel.

"*Non-orthodox people come into our Chapel and cannot understand why all the icons are there. They ask if we have many gods. Then we answer: No, but see there (pointing) is Christ and He said, 'Where I am there shall ye be also', so why not paint the people as well?*"

106/107 *Christ*, mid 1980s, oil paint on gypsum plaster. Detail of *The Last Supper*, St Silouan's Chapel.

"*Christ Last Supper: He has a look of goodness, without looking at any special point (any specific direction), it is already salvation, and it is not the struggle anymore.*"

Compare with full view of Christ page 105 and with Christ of *The Last Supper* in the Refectory, page 98.

108   *St John the Evangelist*, mid 1980s, oil paint on gypsum plaster. Detail of *The Last Supper*, St Silouan's Chapel.

"*Use the head of the middle Angel from the Trinity in the Refectory for St John, but not the angel's hair.*"

Compare with drawing of same apostle at *The Cross*, page 48.

109   *St Simon*, mid 1980s, oil paint on gypsum plaster. Detail of *The Last Supper*, St Silouan's Chapel.

Compare with painting of same apostle at *The Last Supper* in the Refectory, page 99, top right.

110   *Apostles*, mid 1980s, oil paint on gypsum plaster. Details of *The Last Supper*, St Silouan's Chapel.

Top left: *St James of Zebedee*. See drawing page 73.

Top right: *St Peter*. Compare with painting of St Peter in the Refectory, page 99.

Bottom left: *St Andrew*.

Bottom right: *St Matthew*. Compare with painting of St Matthew in the Refectory, page 99 and drawing page 65.

111   *Apostles*, mid 1980s, oil paint on gypsum plaster. Details of *The Last Supper*, St Silouan's Chapel.

Top left: *St Bartholomew*.

Top right: *St James of Alpheus*. Compare with same apostle page 99.

Bottom left: *St Thaddeus*.

Bottom right: *St Philip*. See drawing page 75.

112/113 *Christ with Elijah and Moses*, mid 1980s, oil paint on gypsum plaster, Mural, St Silouan's Chapel. Top half of *The Transfiguration*.

"*Christ in the Transfiguration is all light, almost no shadows and outlined in white, to give a luminous effect.*"

114/115 *Christ*, mid 1980s, oil paint on gypsum plaster. Detail of mural of *The Crucifixion*, St Silouan's Chapel. Father Sophrony intended this scene to be "*Simple, calm and dignified, with no overdramatic poses or gestures.*"

For drawing see page 47.

116   *The Resurrection*, mid 1980s, oil paint on gypsum plaster, 2.92 x 3 m. Mural, St Silouan's Chapel.

"*When constructing a painting or an icon the lines need to be directed in such a way that their arrangement creates a harmonious unity of shape and movement. In the wall painting of the Resurrection, the line of the arms of Christ falls on Adam and Eve in such a way that everything in the scene is drawn together.*"

"*Christ should stand on the gates of hell, not dance, but stand straight, dignified and victorious. Christ's head should be at the same level as it is on the cross*". (The Crucifixion is the adjacent mural).

Compare with same scene in the Refectory, page 88.

118   *Adam*, mid 1980s, oil paint on gypsum plaster. Detail of *The Resurrection*, St Silouan's Chapel.

"*We must make the faces of Adam and Eve beautiful, because they are the image of the first creation, especially Eve should be beautiful, Adam loved her, he preferred her to the lions, camels and birds.*"

See drawing page 52.

119   *Eve*, mid 1980s, oil paint on gypsum plaster. Detail of *The Resurrection*, St Silouan's Chapel.

"*The faces (on the murals of the Chapel) can be sculpted with light sandpapering.*" Father Sophrony was very fond of the natural colour of the gypsum plaster, which had a soft pink tinge to it. He liked to use it bare wherever possible, as it is very difficult to paint a rich white with a good surface. For this reason he liked to use it as highlight for the faces as well, by scraping back the colour to reveal the white of the plaster underneath. The effect was one of lightness and transparency.

See drawing page 53.

120   *Christ*, mid 1980s, oil paint on gypsum plaster. Detail of *The Dormition of the Mother of God*, St Silouan's Chapel.

This face was painted in one sitting, as the access to the wall proved to be too difficult because of it being situated very high up. As such it has a unique freshness and spontaneity.

121   *Mother of God*, mid 1980s, oil paint on gypsum plaster. Detail of *The Ascension*, St Silouan's Chapel.

"*We are searching for **spiritual** beauty.*"

122   *Christ with the soul of the Mother of God*, mid 1980s, oil paint on gypsum plaster. Detail of *The Dormition of the Mother of God*, St Silouan's Chapel.

See comment for page 120.

123   *Angel and Apostles*, mid 1980s, oil paint on gypsum plaster.

Detail of *The Ascension*, St Silouan's Chapel.

Top row, from left to right: Andrew, James of Alpheus, Philip.

Bottom row, from left to right: Paul, Bartholomew, John. In comparison with pages 110-111, the same characteristics are kept, but they are less refined as on a smaller scale. For St John, see page 108. For St Paul, see drawing page 70.

124   *St Matthew*, mid 1980s, oil paint on gypsum plaster. Detail of mural of *Pentecost*, St Silouan's Chapel.

Compare with same apostle at *The Last Supper* pages 99 and 110, as well as drawing page 65.

125   *St Paul*, mid 1980s, oil paint on gypsum plaster. Detail of mural of *Pentecost*, St Silouan's Chapel.

For drawing see page 70. Same drawing used for St Paul on page 123.

126/127   *Row of Ascetics*, mid 1980s, oil paint on gypsum plaster. Mural, west wall, St Silouan's Chapel.

From left to right: Sts Macarius, Sisoes, Anthony, Silouan, Poemen, Arsenius, Paissius.

For drawing of St Arsenius, see page 51, of St Paissius, see page 50.

This was originally painted before St Silouan was glorified. The halo was added and the inscription of his name changed in 1988. The saints chosen were those of similar ascetic experience to St Silouan.

See page 60 for the preparatory drawing and page 142/143 for the icon at the iconostasis.

128   *St Silouan*, mid 1980s, oil paint on gypsum plaster. Detail of mural with *Row of Ascetics*, St Silouan's Chapel.

As this was the first time Father Sophrony had painted his elder in full face, he used the techniques he had acquired as a portrait painter. Later when painting the icon for the iconostasis, he used a stricter stylized form.

For the whole mural, see pages 126/127. For drawing see page 60.

129   *Two Ascetics*, mid 1980s, oil paint on gypsum plaster. Detail of mural with *Ascetics*, St Silouan's Chapel.

These two saints are either end of the row, not visible in the illustration on pages 126/127.

Left: *St Nilus of Sora.*

Right: *St Seraphim of Sarov.*

All the saints in this row are drawn in proportion with each other using the same grid, with the exception of St Seraphim, *"We cannot change St Seraphim's character, let him have a broader face than the others."*

Father Sophrony made some experiments to give these two Russian saints blue eyes, see also St James of Alpheus in the Refectory, page 99.

However he never managed this with St Silouan whose eyes were in fact blue.

130/131   *Mother of God*, early 1960s, egg tempera on gesso, 190 x 155cm.

"We should arrive at painting the icons as works of art, and the faces human, not over 'transfigured'."
For full icon see page 146.

132   *St Panteleimon*, 60s/70s, egg tempera on gesso, 56.5cm x 53.3cm. Icon for iconostasis, St John's Chapel, Community of St John the Baptist.

There was a plan to have the icon on the north side on the iconostasis in St John's Chapel with interchangeable icons. As with the case of many of the ideas, this project was only partly carried out.

133   *St Andrew*, 60s/70s, egg tempera on gesso, 56.5cm x 53.3cm.

This icon too, was painted for the north position on the iconostasis in St John's Chapel.

134/135   *St Andrew*, 60s/70s, egg tempera on gesso, 101.5 x 78.8 cm.

Father Sophrony had great veneration for the apostle Andrew and painted him several times: *"I would like a great icon for St Andrew. He was the first called by Christ and it was on his feast that I experienced my first all night vigil as a monk."*

136/137   *Christ the Almighty*, 1970/1980s, egg tempera on gesso, 100cm x 137.5 cm. Mural icon for east wall of All Saints Church, Tolleshunt Knights.

Every winter when the church was not in use, this icon was brought back to the monastery. Father Sophrony continued to work on it a little more almost every winter, but never quite found the expression he wanted.

"Some people have fixed faces, which hardly change at all, other's change all the time. Christ's face was like that – every second it was different."

138/139   *Prophet Moses receiving the Law*, 1985, egg tempera on gesso, 68 x 44 cm.

Father Sophrony had a particular regard for Moses through whom mankind was given the surpassing revelation of God as a Person. He took great pains over the icon, directing every detail of the work and painted the main features himself.

See drawings on pages 44 and 45.

140/141   *St Sophrony of Jerusalem*, 60s/70s, egg tempera on gesso, 106.7 x 74.5cm.

This icon took Father Sophrony several years to complete in the search to find the appropriate expression for his patron saint: an eagle-like, all-seeing look, fitting for a bishop and a pastor of the church.

See drawing page 59.

142/143   *St Silouan the Athonite*, 1988, egg tempera on gesso, 104 x 80cm. Iconostasis, St Silouan's Chapel.

It is a hard task to paint icons of saints where photographs of them exist as there is a natural tendency to copy their external likeness. In this icon the portrait of St Silouan took on a more definite iconographic form.

Compare with drawing and mural on pages 60 and 128.

144/145 *St Helen of Colchester,* 60s/70s, egg tempera on gesso, 201 x 155cm.

For drawing of face, see pages 55 and 56. For lettering see page 161.

This icon was a commission for a church in Colchester, the nearest town to the monastery. St Helen is the patron saint of Colchester, as some sources suggest she was born there, a Roman town at the time.

146 *Mother of God,* early 1960s, mural icon, egg tempera on gesso, 190 x 155cm.

This icon was painted for the chimney breast in the study of the Old Rectory, with a calculated distortion, so as to be seen from the desk opposite. The photo reproduced here was taken from this angle, to look as it was intended to be seen.

"In the icon of the Mother of God I have tried to express her spiritual beauty. When one looks at her, one is drawn to her and in no way repelled. She is strict, but also there is a great gentleness."

148 *Christ in Glory,* 1972, egg tempera on gesso, 2.133 x 1.524 m. Welling, Church of St Michael.

This icon demonstrates the early formation of Father Sophrony's education in post revolutionary Moscow. There are underlying structures and dynamic designs which are not visible at a first glance, but become evident on close examination. Each line and structure is carefully composed and in balance with the whole work. The abstract elements add to the strength of the icon.

The original altar painting was destroyed in the war, and Father Sophrony was commissioned to paint the icon to fit the existing frame.

For the drawing of the face see pages 21 and 24. For details and studies of other parts of the icon see pages 30 - 34.

150/151 Details from *Christ in Glory,* 1972, egg tempera on gesso.

For full icon see page 149, for drawings and studies of some details see pages 30 – 34.

152/153 Details of Letter blocks for Russian edition of *Staretz Silouan,* 1952, Etched metal blocks, size 2.1 x 1.7 cm x 2.3 cm high.

For full range, see page 162.

155 Face of *Archangel Gabriel,* 1985, embroidery, overall size: 206 x 85.5cm. Detail of standing figure of *Archangel Gabriel.* South door of iconostasis, St Silouan's Chapel.

Father Sophrony directed the work and chose the colouring. Note the colour of the eyes.

For full embroidery, see page 103.

156 Reverse of face of *Archangel Gabriel,* embroidery, overall size: 206 x 85.5cm. Detail of standing figure of *Archangel Gabriel,* South door of iconostasis, St Silouan's Chapel.

When the embroidery was completed, Father Sophrony thought the back had a more painterly quality than the front and arranged to have it exposed and protected by glass.

158 Abbreviation of *Christ, XC,* pencil on paper, 17.1 x 15.8 cm. Design for inscription on an icon of Christ.

"To draw a beautiful letter is difficult, it requires much work."

159 Inscriptions for icon of *St Sophrony of Jerusalem,* pencil on paper, 7.6 x 6.3 cm (average).

For finished icon see page 140.

160 Designs for inscription for icon of *Christ the Almighty,* 1970s, pencil and pen on paper, 27 x 21 cm and 58.2 x 9 cm.

"The inscriptions should be just about legible, requiring some effort to read so that it may be remembered, unlike advertisements which one reads unconsciously, automatically."

For finished icon see page 136/137.

161 Inscriptions on icons.

Far left: Drawing of inscription for icon of St Helen, pencil and red pen on paper, 53 x 19.3 cm.

Next: painting of same inscription on finished icon.

For full icon, see page 144.

Right: inscriptions on icon of St Andrew, gold leaf on top of egg tempera on gesso.

For full icon see page 134.

162 Letter blocks and decorative pattern for first Russian edition of *Staretz Silouan,* Paris, 1952, etched metal, single letters 2.1 x 1.7 cm, wider letters 2.2 x 1.7 cm, all 2.3 cm high, decorative frieze 2.8 x 16.3 cm, 2.3 cm high.

"The two great arts are: typography (letters) and iconography."

164/165 Printing block of letter *B* and its printed impression, etched copper mounted on wood, 2.4 x 2.2 cm, 2.4 cm high.

Capital letter for chapter 5, page 55, Russian edition of *Staretz Silouan,* Paris, 1952.

166/167 Printing block of letter *Ж* and its printed impression, etched metal, 2.2 x 1.7 cm x 2.3 cm high,

Capital letter for chapter 13, page 103, Russian edition of *Staretz Silouan,* Paris, 1952.

168/169 Front page of Russian edition of *Staretz Silouan,* 1952, Paris, as printing block and printed impression with dedication by Father Sophrony, etched metal mounted on wood, 23.3 x 16.2 cm, 2.3 cm high.

Inscription in Father Sophrony's own hand:

To still young Maria
Archimandrite Sophrony
With every blessing, with many prayers and love
6ᵗʰ February, 1983.

"The Holy Spirit instructs us in the humility of Christ, that the soul may ever carry within her the Divine grace which gladdens the soul"

St. Silouan, page 161.

170/171   Stavropegic Cross, 1969, wrought iron, 98cm high. Drive of the Monastery, The Old Rectory, Tolleshunt Knights.

         This cross, the symbol of the Monastery, was designed by Father Sophrony and crafted by an artist blacksmith near Manassia Monastery in Serbia. It represents Christ, the cross, standing on the earth, the globe, with its foot resting on the location of Jerusalem. This is to symbolize Christ having conquered the world, both material, the globe, and that which is immaterial, the spiritual, represented by spheres and upturned arches round the globe. Although frequently a connection is made with the Jewish candle stick, in fact it bears no relation to it.

172   Carpet with dynamic design, mid 1970s, woolen tapestry, 2.14 x 1.06 m. Carpet at Royal Doors, St John's Chapel, The Old Rectory.

         The design illustrates the meeting point that takes place at the Royal Doors.

173   Carpet with concentric rings, woolen tapestry, 2.56 x 1.62 m. Carpet at Royal Doors, St Silouan's Chapel.

         The design of the altar carpet echoes constructive designs throughout the Chapel, reflected especially in the ceiling, but also in the *Last Supper*.

174   Ceiling design, 1983, gold leaf, bronze paint, oil paint and bare gypsum plaster. St Silouan's Chapel.

         The ceiling bears the same circular designs as on the carpet, creating an illusion of a domed ceiling.

175   East view of St Silouan's Chapel.

         The designs and movements are reflected in all aspects, forming a general whole with an underlying dynamic circular design.

ACKNOWLEDGMENTS

This book would not have come about without the help of
John Bowlt, Mark Edwards, Father Andrew Louth,
Effie Mavromihali, John Milner, Nina Papadopoulos,
Philippa Steer, Michael Stonelake, Mary Winterer-Papatassos
and the continual support and encouragement of Father Zacharias.

CPSIA information can be obtained
at www.ICGtesting.com
Printed in the USA
LVHW070045221119
638068LV00009B/1275/P